Happenings

Happenings

New Poems for Schools

edited by

MAURICE WOLLMAN

&

DAVID GRUGEON
Honeywell Primary School, Battersea

GEORGE G. HARRAP & CO. LTD
London Toronto Wellington Sydney

First published in Great Britain 1964
by GEORGE G. HARRAP & CO. LTD
182 High Holborn, London, W.C.1

Reprinted: 1966; 1967; 1969

SBN 245 57118 3

*Composed in Walbaum type and printed in Great Britain by
Western Printing Services Ltd, Bristol
Made in Great Britain*

Preface

WE hope you like these poems. There are all sorts here—strange and fantastic, quiet and sad, beautiful, rumbustious, and just plain enjoyable. The people who write these poems are very varied. Some write a new poem every day, some take a year before a new poem comes to them. But, although each poet is a different person, they all have one thing in common: they record in their poems happenings that are important to them. As they write, all their senses are awake and alert. That is why their poems interest us so much. We seem to see things more clearly when a poet writes about what happens to him. The things that happen are not always pleasant to write about. But good poets are honest and they tell us what they see.

It's the same with a photographer. He may stand around all day, waiting for the right moment. Another day, he may return with a hoard of excellent photographs. He is another person who records happenings. The photographers, like the poets in this book, are interested in life around us.

Try writing some poems yourself. Perhaps you already keep your own in a special folder or book. You may get some ideas from the poems in this book. And you may find that one of the photographs starts off a new poem in your mind. Write it down, before you lose it. That way it doesn't just disappear. It becomes a recorded happening—a poem.

M.W.
D.G.

Acknowledgments

Thanks are due to the following for kind permission to print the poems included in this anthology:

W. H. Auden and Messrs Faber and Faber, Ltd, for poem from *Collected Shorter Poems, 1930–1944*; Edmund Blunden and Messrs William Collins, Sons and Co., Ltd, for poem from *Poems of Many Years*; Alan Brownjohn and the Digby Press, for poem from *The Railings*; Charles Causley and Messrs Rupert Hart-Davis, Ltd, for poems from *Union Street*; Peter Champkin for 'Jingle', and Messrs Robert Hale, Ltd, for poem from *Poems of Our Time*; e. e. cummings and Messrs Faber and Faber, Ltd, for poems from *Selected Poems*; the Literary Trustees of Walter de la Mare and the Society of Authors as their representative and Messrs Faber and Faber, Ltd, for poems from *Inward Companion* and *The Burning Glass*; Paul Dehn and Jacques Prévert and Messrs Hamish Hamilton, Ltd, for poem from *Romantic Landscape*; Clifford Dyment and Messrs J. M. Dent and Sons, Ltd, for poem from *Experiences and Places*; T. S. Eliot and Messrs Faber and Faber, Ltd, for poem from *Old Possum's Book of Practical Cats*; Eleanor Farjeon and Messrs Michael Joseph, Ltd, for poem from *Silver, Sand and Snow*; Elizabeth Fleming and Messrs W. Blackie and Sons, Ltd, for poem; the Executors of Robert Frost, Messrs Jonathan Cape, Ltd, and Messrs Holt, Rinehart and Winston, Inc., for poems from *The Complete Poems of Robert Frost*; John Fuller and Messrs Chatto and Windus, Ltd, for poem from *Fairground Music*; Robert Graves and International Authors N. V., and Messrs Cassell and Co., Ltd, for 'The General Elliott' from *Collected Poems, 1959*, and 'The Two Witches' from *More Poems, 1961*; Thom Gunn and Messrs Faber and Faber, Ltd, for poem from *The Sense of Movement*; Donald Hall, for poem; Philip Hobsbaum, for poem; Ted Hughes and Messrs Faber and Faber, Ltd, for poem from *Meet My Folks*; Geoffrey Johnson, for poem; James Kirkup and the Oxford University Press, for poem from *Refusal to Conform*; Christopher Leach, for poem; Christopher Logue and Messrs Hutchinson and Co. (Publishers), Ltd, for poem from *Songs*; Irene McLeod, for poem; Ogden Nash and Messrs J. M. Dent and Sons, Ltd, for poem from *The Private Dining-room*; Ezra Pound and Messrs Faber and Faber, Ltd, for poem from *Selected Poems*; Jacques Prévert, for poems from *Paroles*, © Editions Gallimard; James Reeves and Messrs William Heinemann, Ltd, for poems from *The Wandering Moon, Ragged Robin* and *Prefabulous Animiles*; Theodore Roethke and Messrs A. M. Heath and Co., Ltd and Messrs Secker and Warburg, Ltd, for poems from *Words for the Wind*; Vernon Scannell and *The Listener*, for poem; Ian Serraillier and the Oxford University Press, for poems from *Happily Ever After*; Stevie Smith and Messrs André Deutsch, Ltd, for poems from *Not Waving but Drowning*; A. D. Peters and Messrs Hamish Hamilton, Ltd, for poem from *Selected Poems* by L. A. G. Strong; Hal Summers, for poem; Mrs Edward Thomas and Messrs Faber and Faber, Ltd, for poem from *Collected Poems* by Edward Thomas; R. S. Thomas and Messrs Rupert Hart-Davis, Ltd, for poem from *Song at the Year's Turning*; Anthony Thwaite and the Oxford University Press, for poem from *The Owl in the Tree*; Michael Thwaites and Messrs Putnam and Co., Ltd, for extract from poem from *The Jervis Bay*; J. R. R. Tolkien and Messrs George Allen and Unwin, Ltd, for poems from *The Adventures of Tom Bombadil*; Henry Treece and Messrs Faber and Faber, Ltd, for poem from *The Black Seasons*; the Executors of W. J. Turner and Messrs Sidgwick and Jackson, Ltd, for poem from *The Hunter*; John Updike and Messrs Victor Gollancz, Ltd, for poem from *Hoping for a Hoopoe*; Arthur Waley and Messrs Allen and Unwin, Ltd, for poems from *Chinese Poems*; Robert Wallace and *The New Yorker* and Scribners' *Poems of Today IV*, for poem; Rex Warner and Messrs John Lane (The Bodley Head), Ltd, for poem from *Poems* (Boriswood); the Executors of W. Carlos Williams and *New Directions*, for poems from *Collected Earlier Poems*; Andrew Young and Messrs Rupert Hart-Davis, Ltd, for poem from *Collected Poems*. The editors regret that they have been unable to contact Mr Stanley Chapman, who translated the poem *Whale Hunt*, by Jacques Prévert, which appeared in *Stand*.

The cover photograph is by Michael Taylor, Shell-Mex and B.P., Ltd, and is reproduced by permission of the Provost and Chapter of Coventry Cathedral.

Nine of the photographs in this book are by Roger Mayne and three (opposite pages 32, 49, and 81) are by J. Allan Cash. We should like to record our pleasure in finding photographers who approach the spirit of these poems so closely.

Contents

Anne and the Field-mouse

Ian Serraillier

WE found a mouse in the chalk quarry today
In a circle of stones and empty oil drums
By the fag ends of a fire. There had been
A picnic there; he must have been after the crumbs.

Jane saw him first, a flicker of brown fur
In and out of the charred wood and chalk-white.
I saw him last, but not till we'd turned up
Every stone and surprised him into flight,

Though not far—little zigzag spurts from stone
To stone. Once, as he lurked in his hiding-place,
I saw his beady eyes uplifted to mine.
I'd never seen such terror in so small a face.

I watched, amazed and guilty. Beside us suddenly
A heavy pheasant whirred up from the ground,
Scaring us all; and, before we knew it, the mouse
Had broken cover, skimming away without a sound,

Melting into the nettles. We didn't go
Till I'd chalked in capitals on a rusty can:
THERE'S A MOUSE IN THOSE NETTLES. LEAVE
HIM ALONE. NOVEMBER 15th. ANNE.

◇◇◇◇

The Red Cockatoo

Arthur Waley

(FROM THE CHINESE)

SENT as a present from Annam—
A red cockatoo.
Coloured like the peach-tree blossom,
Speaking with the speech of men.
And they did to it what is always done
To the learned and eloquent.
They took a cage with stout bars
And shut it up inside.

◇◇◇◇

My Sister Jane

Ted Hughes

AND I say nothing—no, not a word
About our Jane. Haven't you heard?
She's a bird, a bird, a bird, a bird.
Oh it never would do to let folks know
My sister's nothing but a great big crow.

Each day (we daren't send her to school)
She pulls on stockings of thick blue wool
To make her pin crow legs look right,
Then fits a wig of curls on tight,

And dark spectacles—a huge pair
To cover her very crowy stare.
Oh it never would do to let folks know
My sister's nothing but a great big crow.

When visitors come she sits upright
(With her wings and her tail tucked out of sight).
They think her queer but extremely polite.
Then when the visitors have gone
She whips out her wings and with her wig on
Whirls through the house at the height of your head—
Duck, duck, or she'll knock you dead.
Oh it never would do to let folks know
My sister's nothing but a great big crow.

At meals whatever she sees she'll stab it—
Because she's a crow and that's a crow habit.
My mother says 'Jane! Your manners! Please!'
Then she'll sit quietly on the cheese,
Or play the piano nicely by dancing on the keys—
Oh it never would do to let folks know
My sister's nothing but a great big crow.

❖❖❖❖

Hedgehog

Anthony Thwaite

TWITCHING the leaves just where the drainpipe
  clogs
In ivy leaves and mud, a purposeful
Creature at night about its business. Dogs
Fear his stiff seriousness. He chews away

At beetles, worms, slugs, frogs. Can kill a hen
With one snap of his jaws, can taunt a snake
To death on muscled spines. Old countrymen
Tell tales of hedgehogs sucking a cow dry.

But this one, cramped by houses, fences, walls,
Must have slept here all winter in that heap
Of compost, or have inched by intervals
Through tidy gardens to this ivy bed.

And here, dim-eyed, but ears so sensitive
A voice within the house can make him freeze,
He scuffs the edge of danger: yet can live
Happily in our nights and absences.

A country creature, wary, quiet and shrewd,
He takes the milk we give him, when we're gone.
At night, our slamming voices must seem crude
To one who sits and waits for silences.

◇◇◇◇

maggie and milly and molly and may

e. e. cummings

maggie and milly and molly and may
went down to the beach (to play one day)

and maggie discovered a shell that sang
so sweetly she couldn't remember her troubles, and

milly befriended a stranded star
whose rays five languid fingers were;

and molly was chased by a horrible thing
which raced sideways while blowing bubbles: and

may came home with a smooth round stone
as small as a world and as large as alone.

For whatever we lose (like a you or a me)
it's always ourselves we find in the oca

◇◇◇◇

Growltiger's Last Stand

T. S. Eliot

GROWLTIGER was a Bravo Cat, who travelled on
   a barge:
In fact he was the roughest cat that ever roamed at large.
From Gravesend up to Oxford he pursued his evil aims,
Rejoicing in his title of 'The Terror of the Thames'.

His manners and appearance did not calculate to please;
His coat was torn and seedy, he was baggy at the knees;
One ear was somewhat missing, no need to tell you why,
And he scowled upon a hostile world from one
   forbidding eye.

The cottagers of Rotherhithe knew something of his
   fame;
At Hammersmith and Putney people shuddered at his
   name.

They would fortify the hen-house, lock up the silly
    goose,
When the rumour ran along the shore:
    GROWLTIGER'S ON THE LOOSE!

Woe to the weak canary, that fluttered from its cage;
Woe to the pampered Pekinese, that faced
    Growltiger's rage;
Woe to the bristly Bandicoot, that lurks on foreign
    ships;
And woe to any Cat with whom Growltiger came to grips!

But most to Cats of foreign race his hatred had been
    vowed;
To Cats of foreign name and race no quarter was
    allowed.
The Persian and the Siamese regarded him with fear—
Because it was a Siamese had mauled his missing ear.

Now on a peaceful summer night, all nature seemed
    at play,
The tender moon was shining bright, the barge at
    Molesey lay.
All in the balmy moonlight it lay rocking on the tide—
And Growltiger was disposed to show his sentimental
    side.

His bucko mate, GRUMBUSKIN, long since had
    disappeared,
For to the Bell at Hampton he had gone to wet his beard;
And his bosun, TUMBLEBRUTUS, he too had stol'n
    away—
In the yard behind the Lion he was prowling for his
    prey.

In the forepeak of the vessel Growltiger sate alone,
Concentrating his attention on the Lady GRIDDLE-
BONE.
And his raffish crew were sleeping in their barrels and
their bunks—
As the Siamese came creeping in their sampans and their
junks.

Growltiger had no eye or ear for aught but Griddlebone,
And the Lady seemed enraptured by his manly
baritone,
Disposed to relaxation, and awaiting no surprise—
But the moonlight shone reflected from a thousand
bright blue eyes.

And closer still and closer the sampans circled round,
And yet from all the enemy there was not heard a sound.
The lovers sang their last duet, in danger of their lives—
For the foe was armed with toasting forks and cruel
carving knives.

Then GILBERT gave the signal to his fierce
Mongolian horde;
With a frightful burst of fireworks the Chinks they
swarmed aboard.
Abandoning their sampans, and their pullaways and
junks,
They battened down the hatches on the crew within
their bunks.

Then Griddlebone she gave a screech, for she was
badly skeered;
I am sorry to admit it, but she quickly disappeared.

She probably escaped with ease, I'm sure she was not
    drowned—
But a serried ring of flashing steel Growltiger did
    surround.

The ruthless foe pressed forward, in stubborn rank on rank;
Growltiger to his vast surprise was forced to walk the
    plank.
He who a hundred victims had driven to that drop
At the end of all his crimes was forced to go ker-flip,
    ker-flop.

Oh there was joy in Wapping when the news flew
    through the land;
At Maidenhead and Henley there was dancing on the
    strand.
Rats were roasted whole at Brentford, and at
    Victoria Dock,
And a day of celebration was commanded in Bangkok.

❖❖❖

Child on Top of a Greenhouse

Theodore Roethke

THE wind billowing out the seat of my britches,
My feet crackling splinters of glass and dried putty,
The half-grown chrysanthemums staring up like
    accusers,
Up through the streaked glass, flashing with sunlight,
A few white clouds all rushing eastward,
A line of elms plunging and tossing like horses,
And everyone, everyone pointing up and shouting!

❖❖❖

How to Paint the Portrait of a Bird

Paul Dehn

(TRANSLATED FROM THE FRENCH OF
JACQUES PRÉVERT)

FIRST paint a cage
with an open door
then paint
something pretty
something simple
something fine
something useful
for the bird
next place the canvas against a tree
in a garden
in a wood
or in a forest
hide behind the tree
without speaking
without moving . . . .
Sometimes the bird comes quickly
but it can also take many years
before making up its mind
Don't be discouraged
wait
wait if necessary for years
the quickness or the slowness of the coming
of the bird having no relation
to the success of the picture
When the bird comes
if it comes
observe the deepest silence
wait for the bird to enter the cage

and when it has entered
gently close the door with the paint-brush
then
one by one paint out all the bars
taking care not to touch one feather of the bird
Next make a portrait of the tree
choosing the finest of its branches
for the bird
paint also the green leaves and the freshness of the
  wind
dust in the sun
and the sound of the grazing cattle in the heat of
  summer
and wait for the bird to decide to sing
If the bird does not sing
it is a bad sign
a sign that the picture is bad
but if it sings it is a good sign
a sign that you are ready to sign
so then you pluck very gently
one of the quills of the bird
and you write your name in a corner of the picture

❖❖❖

Beech Leaves

James Reeves

IN autumn down the beechwood path
  The leaves lie thick upon the ground.
It's there I love to kick my way
  And hear their crisp and crashing sound.

I am a giant, and my steps
　　Echo and thunder to the sky.
How the small creatures of the woods
　　Must quake and cower as I pass by!

This brave and merry noise I make
　　In summer also when I stride
Down to the shining, pebbly sea
　　And kick the frothing waves aside.

⋄-⋄-⋄-⋄

'The General Elliott'

Robert Graves

HE fell in victory's fierce pursuit,
　　Holed through and through with shot;
A sabre sweep had hacked him deep
　　'Twixt neck and shoulder-knot.

The potman cannot well recall,
　　The ostler never knew,
Whether that day was Malplaquet,
　　The Boyne, or Waterloo.

But there he hangs, a tavern sign,
　　With foolish bold regard
For cock and hen and loitering men
　　And wagons down the yard.

Raised high above the hayseed world
　　He smokes his china pipe;
And now surveys the orchard ways,
　　The damsons clustering ripe—

Stares at the churchyard slabs beyond,
Where country neighbours lie:
Their brief renown set lowly down,
But his invades the sky.

He grips a tankard of brown ale
That spills a generous foam:
Often he drinks, they say, and winks
At drunk men lurching home.

No upstart hero may usurp
That honoured swinging seat;
His seasons pass with pipe and glass
Until the tale's complete—

And paint shall keep his buttons bright
Though all the world's forgot
Whether he died for England's pride
By battle or by pot.

❖❖❖

Cynddylan on a Tractor

R. S. Thomas

A H, you should see Cynddylan on a tractor.
Gone the old look that yoked him to the soil;
He's a new man now, part of the machine,
His nerves of metal and his blood oil.
The clutch curses, but the gears obey
His least bidding, and lo, he's away
Out of the farmyard, scattering hens.
Riding to work now as a great man should,
He is the knight at arms breaking the fields'
Mirror of silence, emptying the wood

Of foxes and squirrels and bright jays.
The sun comes over the tall trees
Kindling all the hedges, but not for him
Who runs his engine on a different fuel.
And all the birds are singing, bills wide in vain,
As Cynddylan passes proudly up the lane.

❖❖❖❖

The Term

W. Carlos Williams

A rumpled sheet
of brown paper
about the length

and apparent bulk
of a man was
rolling with the

wind slowly over
and over in
the street as

a car drove down
upon it and
crushed it to

the ground. Unlike
a man it rose
again rolling

with the wind over
and over to be as
it was before.

❖❖❖❖

The Witch's Cat

Ian Serraillier

'MY magic is dead,' said the witch. 'I'm astounded
That people can fly to the moon and around it.
It used to be mine and the cat's till they found it.
My broomstick is draughty, I snivel with cold
As I ride to the stars. I'm painfully old,
    And so is my cat;
    But planet-and-space-ship,
    Rocket or race-ship
Never shall part me from that.'

She wrote an advertisement, 'Witch in a fix
Willing to part with the whole bag of tricks,
Going cheap at the price at eighteen and six.'
But no one was ready to empty his coffers
For out-of-date rubbish. There weren't any offers—
    Except for the cat.
    'But planet-and-space-ship,
    Rocket or race-ship
Never shall part me from that.'

The tears trickled fast, not a sentence she spoke
As she stamped on her broom and the brittle stick broke,
And she dumped in a dustbin her hat and her cloak,
Then clean disappeared, leaving no prints;
And no one at all has set eyes on her since
    Or her tired old cat.
    'But planet-and-space-ship,
    Rocket or race-ship
Never shall part me from that.'

◇◇◇

Hide and Seek

Vernon Scannell

Yoo-hoo! I'm ready! Come and find me!

THE sacks in the toolshed smell like the seaside.
You make yourself little in the salty dark,
Close your eyes tight and hope your feet aren't
   showing.
Better not risk another call, they might be close.
Don't sneeze whatever happens. The floor is cold.
They're probably searching the bushes near the swing.
What's that? That sounds like them. They're coming in!
Don't breathe or move. Still. Someone knocks a can.
Feet mutter. Somebody comes very close,
A scuffle of words, a laugh, and then they're gone.
They might be back. Careful in case they come.
They'll try the greenhouse, then in here again.
They're taking a long time, but they'll come back.
Risk a peep out, perhaps? Not yet; they might creep in.
A good hiding-place, this: the best you've ever found.
It's funny, though, they haven't tried again.
Can't hear a thing. They must be miles away.
The dark damp smell of sand is thicker now.
Give them another call: *Yoo-hoo! Come and find me!*
But they are still elsewhere. They'll think you're
   clever,
And ask you where you hid. Don't tell them. Keep
   it secret.
It's cold in here. You can't hear anything.
But wait. Let them hunt a little longer;
Think of them frowning at each other:
Where can he be? We've looked all over.
Something tickles on your nose. Your legs are stiff.

Just a little longer and then creep out.
They're not coming back. You've tricked them
   properly.
All right. Push off the sacks. That's better.
Good to be rid of that unpleasant smell.
Out of the shed. *Hey! Here I am! I'm here!*
I've won the game! You couldn't find me!
The darkening garden watches. Nothing stirs.
The bushes hold their breath. The air is cold.
Yes, here you are, but where are they who sought you?

◇◇◇

Nile Fishermen

Rex Warner

NAKED men, fishing in Nile without a licence,
kneedeep in it, pulling gaunt at stretched ropes.
Round the next bend is the police boat and the
   officials
ready to make an arrest on the yellow sand.

The splendid bodies are stark to the swimming sand,
taut to the ruffled water, the flickering palms,
yet swelling and quivering as they tug at the
   trembling ropes.
Their faces are bent along the arms and still.

Sun is torn in coloured petals on the water,
the water shivering in the heat and the north wind;
and near and far billow out white swollen crescents,
the clipping wings of feluccas, seagull sails.

A plunge in the turbid water, a quick joke stirs
a flashing of teeth, an invocation of God
Here is food to be fetched and living from labour.
The tight ropes strain and the glittering backs for the
    haul.

Round the bend comes the police boat. The men
    scatter.
The officials blow their whistles on the golden
    sand.
They overtake and arrest strong bodies of men
who follow with sullen faces, and leave their nets
    behind.

❖❖❖

Who's In

Elizabeth Fleming

'THE door is shut fast
And everyone's out.'
But people don't know
What they're talking about!
Says the fly on the wall,
And the flame on the coals
And the dog on his rug
And the mice in their holes,
And the kitten curled up,
And the spiders that spin—
'What, everyone's out?
Why, everyone's in!'

❖❖❖

Nursery Rhyme of Innocence and Experience

Charles Causley

I HAD a silver penny
And an apricot tree
And I said to the sailor
On the white quay

'Sailor O sailor
Will you bring me
If I give you my penny
And my apricot tree

'A fez from Algeria
An Arab drum to beat
A little gilt sword
And a parakeet?'

And he smiled and he kissed me
As strong as death
And I saw his red tongue
And I felt his sweet breath

'*You may keep your penny*
And your apricot tree
And I'll bring your presents
Back from sea.'

O the ship dipped down
On the rim of the sky
And I waited while three
Long summers went by

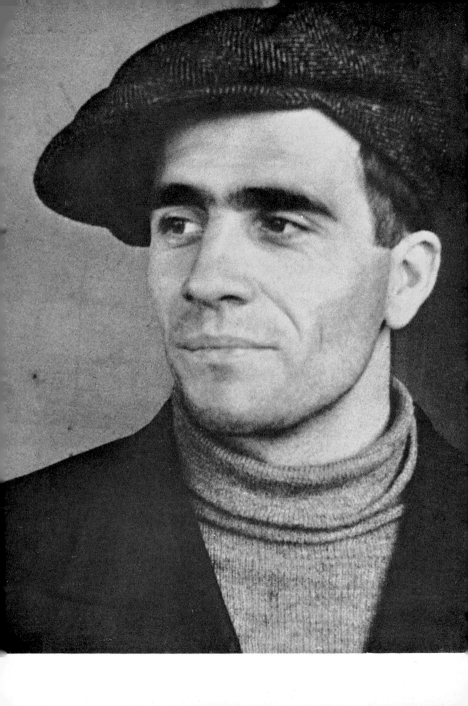

Then one steel morning
   On the white quay
I saw a grey ship
   Come in from sea

Slowly she came
   Across the bay
For her flashing rigging
   Was shot away

All round her wake
   The seabirds cried
And flew in and out
   Of the hole in her side

Slowly she came
   In the path of the sun
And I heard the sound
   Of a distant gun

And a stranger came running
   Up to me
From the deck of the ship
   And he said, said he

'*O are you the boy*
   Who would wait on the quay
With the silver penny
   And the apricot tree?

'*I've a plum-coloured fez*
   And a drum for thee
And a sword and a parakeet
   From over the sea.'

'O where is the sailor
With bold red hair?
And what is that volley
On the bright air?

'O where are the other
Girls and boys?
And why have you brought me
Children's toys?'

The Idlers

Edmund Blunden

THE gipsies lit their fires by the chalk-pits anew,
And the hoppled horses supped in the further dusk
and dew;
The gnats flocked round the smoke like idlers as they
were
And through the goss and bushes the owls began to
churr.

An ell above the woods the last of sunset glowed
With a dusky gold that filled the pond beside the road;
The cricketers had done, the leas all silent lay,
And the carrier's clattering wheels went past and
died away.

The gipsies lolled and gossipped, and ate their stolen
swedes,
Made merry with mouth-organs, worked toys with
piths of reeds:

The old wives puffed their pipes, nigh as black as
   their hair,
And not one of them all seemed to know the name of
   care.

◇◇◇◇

A bird came down the walk

Emily Dickinson

A BIRD came down the walk.
He did not know I saw.
He bit an angleworm in halves
And ate the fellow raw,

And then he drank a dew
From a convenient grass,
And then hopped sidewise to the wall
To let a beetle pass.

He glanced with rapid eyes
That hurried all around;
They looked like frightened beads, I thought;
He stirred his velvet head

Like one in danger, cautious;
I offered him a crumb,
And he unrolled his feathers
And rode him softer home

Than oars divide the ocean,
Too silver for a seam,
Or butterflies off banks of noon
Leap, plashless as they swim.

◇◇◇◇

To See the Rabbit

Alan Brownjohn

WE are going to see the rabbit.
We are going to see the rabbit.
Which rabbit, people say?
Which rabbit, ask the children?
Which rabbit?
The only rabbit,
The only rabbit in England,
Sitting behind a barbed-wire fence
Under the floodlights, neon lights,
Sodium lights,
Nibbling grass
On the only patch of grass
In England, in England
(Except the grass by the hoardings
Which doesn't count).
We are going to see the rabbit
And we must be there on time.

First we shall go by escalator,
Then we shall go by underground,
And then we shall go by motorway,
And then by helicopterway,
And the last ten yards we shall have to go
On foot.

And now we are going
All the way to see the rabbit,
We are nearly there,
We are longing to see it,
And so is the crowd

Which is here in thousands
With mounted policemen
And big loudspeakers
And bands and banners,
And everyone has come a long way.

But soon we shall see it
Sitting and nibbling
The blades of grass
On the only patch of grass
In—but something has gone wrong!
Why is everyone so angry,
Why is everyone jostling
And slanging and complaining?

The rabbit has gone,
Yes, the rabbit has gone.
He has actually burrowed down into the earth
And made himself a warren, under the earth,
Despite all these people,
And what shall we do?
What *can* we do?

It is all a pity, you must be disappointed,
Go home and do something else for today,
Go home again, go home for today.
For you cannot hear the rabbit, under the earth,
Remarking rather sadly to himself, by himself,
As he rests in his warren, under the earth:
'It won't be long, they are bound to come,
They are bound to come and find me, even here.'

◇◇◇

The Lonely Scarecrow

James Kirkup

MY poor old bones—I've only two—
A broomshank and a broken stave.
My ragged gloves are a disgrace.
My one peg-foot is in the grave.

I wear the labourer's old clothes:
Coat, shirt and trousers all undone.
I bear my cross upon a hill
In rain and shine, in snow and sun.

I cannot help the way I look.
My funny hat is full of hay.
—O, wild birds, come and nest in me!
Why do you always fly away?

◇◇◇◇

Stopping by Woods on a Snowy Evening

Robert Frost

WHOSE woods these are I think I know.
His house is in the village though;
He will not see me stopping here
To watch his woods fill up with snow.

My little horse must think it queer
To stop without a farmhouse near
Between the woods and frozen lake
The darkest evening of the year.

He gives his harness bells a shake
To ask if there is some mistake.
The only other sound's the sweep
Of easy wind and downy flake.

The woods are lovely, dark and deep,
But I have promises to keep,
And miles to go before I sleep,
And miles to go before I sleep.

❖❖❖❖

Ballad

Henry Treece

OH come, my joy, my soldier boy,
With your golden buttons, your scarlet coat,
Oh let me play with your twinkling sword
And sail away in your wonderful boat!

The soldier came and took the boy.
Together they marched the dusty roads.
Instead of war, they sang at Fairs,
And mended old chairs with river reeds.

The boy put on a little black patch
And learned to sing on a tearful note;
The soldier sold his twinkling sword
To buy a crutch and a jet-black flute.

And when the summer sun rode high
They laughed the length of the shining day;
But when the robin stood in the hedge
The little lad's courage drained away.

Oh soldier, my soldier, take me home
To the nut-brown cottage under the hill.
My mother is waiting, I'm certain sure;
She's far too old to draw at the well!

As snowflakes fell the boy spoke so,
For twenty years, ah twenty years;
But a look in the soldier's eyes said no,
And the roads of England were wet with tears.

One morning, waking on the moors,
The lad laughed loud at the corpse by his side.
He buried the soldier under a stone,
But kept the flute to soothe his pride.

The days dragged on and he came to a town,
Where he got a red jacket for chopping wood;
And meeting a madman by the way,
He bartered the flute for a twinkling sword.

And so he walked the width of the land
With a warlike air and a jaunty word,
Looking out for a likely lad,
With the head of a fool and the heart of a bard.

⟡⟡⟡

Our Local Zoo

Geoffrey Johnson

EXPERT officials at our Zoo
From long research at Timbuctoo
Conclude our winter's much too keen
For creatures of the tropic scene

And have provided woollen pants
For giraffes and elephants,
Vests for the chimpanzees, and bloomers
To fit the more fastidious pumas.
Loud is the crowd in cacchination
At this fantastic innovation,
And yet not more fantastic is it
Than many folk who pay their visit
In garbs of immemorial habit
In furs of fox and stoat and rabbit,
In leopard pantaloons *et al.*,
Peculiar to the animal,
And never feel uncertainty
Which side the bars they ought to be.

◇◇◇◇

The Two Witches

Robert Graves

O SIXTEEN hundred and ninety one,
Never was year so well begun,
Backsy-forsy and inside-out,
The best of all years to ballad about.

On the first fine day of January
I ran to my sweetheart Margery
And tossed her over the roof so far
That down she fell like a shooting star.

But when we two had frolicked and kissed
She clapped her fingers about my wrist
And tossed me over the chimney stack,
And danced on me till my bones did crack.

Then, when she had laboured to ease my pain,
We sat by the stile of Robin's Lane,
She in a hare and I in a toad
And puffed at the clouds till merry they glowed.

We spelled our loves until close of day.
I wished her good-night and walked away,
But she put out a tongue that was long and red
And swallowed me down like a crumb of bread.

◇◇◇◇

Alex at the Barber's

John Fuller

HE is having his hair cut. Towels are tucked
About his chin, his mop scalped jokingly.
The face in the mirror is his own face.

The barber moves and chats among the green
And methylated violet, snipper-snips,
Puts scissors down, puts in a plaited flex,

And like a surgeon with his perfumed hands
Presses the waiting skull and shapes the base.
He likes having his hair cut, and the man

Likes cutting it. The radio drones on.
The eyes in the mirror are his own eyes.
While the next chair receives the Demon Blade,

A dog-leg razor nicks a sideburn here;
As from a sofa there a sheet is whisked
And silver pocketed. The doorbell pings.

The barber, frowning, grips the ragged fringe
And slowly cuts. Upon the speckled sheet
The bits fall down and now his hair is cut.

The neighing trams outside splash through the rain.
The barber tests the spray for heat and rubs
Lemon shampoo into his spiky hair.

Bent with his head above the running bowl,
Eyes squeezed shut, he does not see the water
Gurgle and sway like twisted sweetpaper

Above the waste, but, for a moment, tows
A sleigh of polished silver parrots through
Acres of snow, exclaiming soundlessly.

Then towel round head. Head swung gently up.
Eyes padded. As the barber briskly rubs,
The smile in the mirror is his own smile.

❖❖❖❖

Lady, weeping at the crossroads

W. H. Auden

LADY, weeping at the crossroads
Would you meet your love
In the twilight with his greyhounds
And the hawk on his glove?

Bribe the birds then on the branches,
Bribe them to be dumb,
Stare the hot sun out of heaven
That the night may come.

Starless are the nights of travel,
Bleak the winter wind;
Run with terror all before you
And regret behind.

Run until you hear the ocean's
Everlasting cry;
Deep though it may be and bitter
You must drink it dry.

Wear out patience in the lowest
Dungeons of the sea,
Searching through the stranded shipwrecks
For the golden key.

Push on to the world's end, pay the
Dread guard with a kiss;
Cross the rotten bridge that totters
Over the abyss.

There stands the deserted castle
Ready to explore;
Enter, climb the marble staircase
Open the locked door.

Cross the silent empty ballroom,
Doubt and danger past;
Blow the cobwebs from the mirror
See yourself at last.

Put your hand behind the wainscot,
You have done your part;
Find the penknife there and plunge it
Into your false heart.

◇◇◇◇

The Hippocrump

James Reeves

ALONG the valley of the Ump
Gallops the fearful Hippocrump.
His hide is leathery and thick;
His eyelids open with a *Click!*
His mouth he closes with a *Clack!*
He has three humps upon his back;
On each of these there grows a score
Of horny spikes, and sometimes more.
His hair is curly, thick and brown;
Beneath his chin a beard hangs down.
He has eight feet with hideous claws;
His neck is long—and O his jaws!
The boldest falters in his track
To hear those hundred teeth go *Clack!*

The Hippocrump is fierce indeed,
But if he eats the baneful weed
That grows beside the Purple Lake,
His hundred teeth begin to ache.
Then how the creature stamps and roars
Along the Ump's resounding shores!
The drowsy cattle faint with fright;
The birds fall flat, the fish turn white.
Even the rocks begin to shake;
The children in their beds awake;
The old ones quiver, quail, and quake.
'Alas!' they cry. 'Make no mistake,
It is *Himself*—he's got the Ache
From eating by the Purple Lake!'
Some say, 'It is *Old You-know-who*—
He's in a rage: what *shall* we do?'

'Lock up the barns, protect the stores,
Bring all the pigs and sheep indoors!'
They call upon their god, Agw-ump
To save them from the Hippocrump.
'What's that I hear go hop-skip-jump?
He's coming! Stand aside there!' *Bump!*
Lump-lump!—'He's on the bridge now!'—*Lump!*
'I hear his tail'—*ker-flump, ker-flump!*
'I see the prickles on his hump!
It *is*, it IS—the Hippocrump!
Defend us now, O Great Agw-ump!'

Thus prayed the dwellers by the Ump.
Their prayer was heard. A broken stump
Caught the intruder in the rump.
He slipped into the foaming river,
Whose icy water quenched his fever,
Then while the creature floundering lay,
The timid people ran away;
And when the morrow dawned serene
The Hippocrump was no more seen.
Glad hymns of joy the people raised:
'For ever Great Agw-ump be praised!'

◇◇◇

The Solitary Poet

Peter Champkin

LONG after the poet has gone
His songs remain in the streets,
In the voices of autumn,
In the noise of vagabonds.

Adventurer, he finds no friend
Or parliament beneath the sun.
His speech is suddenly heard
In a cry, in a word
Long after the poet has gone.

◇◇◇◇

St Martin and the Beggar

Thom Gunn

MARTIN sat young upon his bed
A budding cenobite,
Said 'Though I hold the principles
Of Christian life be right,
I cannot grow from them alone,
I must go out to fight.'

He travelled hard, he travelled far,
The light began to fail.
'Is not this act of mine,' he said,
'A cowardly betrayal,
Should I not peg my nature down
With a religious nail?'

Wind scudded on the marshland,
And, dangling at his side,
His sword soon clattered under hail:
What could he do but ride?—
There was not shelter for a dog,
The garrison far ahead.

A ship that moves on darkness
He rode across the plain,
When a brawny beggar started up
Who pulled at his rein
And leant dripping with sweat and water
Upon the horse's mane.

He glared into Martin's eyes
With eyes more wild than bold;
His hair sent rivers down his spine;
Like a fowl plucked to be sold
His flesh was grey. Martin said—
'What, naked in this cold?

'I have no food to give you,
Money would be a joke.'
Pulling his new sword from the sheath
He took his soldier's cloak
And cut it in two equal parts
With a single stroke.

Grabbing one to his shoulders,
Pinning it with his chin,
The beggar dived into the dark,
And soaking to the skin
Martin went on slowly
Until he reached an inn.

One candle on the wooden table,
The food and drink were poor,
The woman hobbled off, he ate,
Then casually before
The table stood the beggar as
If he had used the door.

Now dry for hair and flesh had been
By warm airs fanned,
Still bare but round each muscled thigh
A single golden band,
His eyes now wild with love, he held
The half cloak in his hand.

'You recognised the human need
Included yours, because
You did not hesitate, my saint,
To cut your cloak across;
But never since that moment
Did you regret the loss.

'My enemies would have turned away,
My holy toadies would
Have given all the cloak and frozen
Conscious that they were good.
But you, being a saint of men,
Gave only what you could.'

St Martin stretched his hand out
To offer from his plate,
But the beggar vanished, thinking food
Like cloaks is needless weight.
Pondering on the matter,
St Martin bent and ate.

❖❖❖

Double Dutch

Walter de la Mare

THAT crafty cat, a buff-black Siamese,
Sniffing through wild wood, sagely, silently goes,
Prick ears, lank legs, alertly twitching nose,
And on her secret errand reads with ease
A language no man knows.

◇◇◇◇

The Owl

Walter de la Mare

OWL of the wildwood I:
Muffled in sleep I drowse,
Where no fierce sun in heaven
Can me arouse.

My haunt's a hollow
In a half-dead tree,
Whose strangling ivy
Shields and shelters me.

But when dark's starlight
Thrids my green domain,
My plumage trembles and stirs,
I wake again:

A spectral moon
Silvers the world I see;
Out of their daylong lairs
Creep thievishly

Night's living things.
Then I,
Wafted away on soundless pinions
Fly;
Curdling her arches
With my hunting cry:

A-hooh! a-hooh:
Four notes; and then,
Solemn, sepulchral, cold,
Four notes again,
The listening dingles
Of my woodland through:
A-hooh! A-hooh!
A-hooh!

◇◇◇◇

Jargon

James Reeves

JERUSALEM, Joppa, Jericho—
These are the cities of long ago.

Jasper, jacinth, jet and jade—
Of such are jewels for ladies made.

Juniper's green and jasmine's white,
Sweet jonquil is spring's delight.

Joseph, Jeremy, Jennifer, James,
Julian, Juliet—just names.

January, July and June—
Birthday late or birthday soon.

Jacket, jersey, jerkin, jeans—
What's the wear for sweet sixteens?

Jaguar, jackal, jumbo, jay—
Came to dinner but couldn't stay.

Jellies, junkets, jumbals, jam—
Mix them up for sweet-toothed Sam.

To jig, to jaunt, to jostle, to jest—
These are the things that Jack loves best.

Jazz, jamboree, jubilee, joke—
The jolliest words you ever spoke.

From A to Z and Z to A
The joyfullest letter of all is J.

◇◇◇◇

The Wangsun [1]

Arthur Waley

(FROM THE CHINESE)

SUBLIME was he, stupendous in invention,
Who planned the miracles of earth and sky.
Wondrous the power that charged
Small things with secret beauty, moving in them all.
See now the wangsun, crafty creature, mean of size,
Uncouth of form; the wrinkled face
Of an aged man; the body of a little child.
See how in turn he blinks and blenches with an air
Pathetically puzzled, dimly gazes
Under tired lids, through languid lashes

[1] A kind of small, tailless ape (?)

Looks tragic and hollow-eyed, rumples his brow,
Scatters this way and that
An insolent, astonished glare;
Sniffs and snorts, snuffs and sneezes,
Snicks and cocks his knowing little ears!
Now like a dotard mouths and chews
Or hoots and hisses through his pouted lips;
Shows gnashing teeth, grates and grinds ill-temperedly,
Gobbles and puffs and scolds.
And every now and then,
Down to his belly, from the lardor that he keeps
In either cheek, he sends
Little consignments lowered cautiously.
Sometimes he squats
Like a puppy on its haunches, or hare-like humps
An arching back;
Smirks and wheedles with ingratiating sweetness;
Or suddenly takes to whining, surly snarling;
Then, like a ravening tiger roars.

He lives in thick forests, deep among the hills,
Or houses in the clefts of sharp, precipitous rocks;
Alert and agile is his nature, nimble are his wits;
Swift are his contortions,
Apt to every need,
Whether he climb tall tree-stems of a hundred feet,
Or sways on the shuddering shoulder of a long bough.
Before him, the dark gullies of unfathomable streams;
Behind, the silent hollows of the lonely hills.
Twigs and tendrils are his rocking-chairs,
On rungs of rotting wood he trips
Up perilous places; sometimes, leap after leap,
Like lightning flits through the woods.
Sometimes he saunters with a sad, forsaken air;

Then suddenly peeps round,
Beaming with satisfaction. Up he springs,
Leaps and prances, whoops, and scampers on his way.
Up cliffs he scrambles, up pointed rocks,
Dances on shale that shifts or twigs that snap,
Suddenly swerves and lightly passes . . .
Oh, what tongue could unravel
The tale of all his tricks?

Alas, one trait
With the human tribe he shares; their sweet's his sweet,
Their bitter is his bitter. Off sugar from the vat
Or brewer's dregs he loves to sup.
So men put wine where he will pass.
How he races to the bowl!
How nimbly licks and swills!
Now he staggers, feels dazed and foolish,
Darkness falls upon his eyes . . . .
He sleeps and knows no more.
Up steal the trappers, catch him by the mane,
Then to a string or ribbon tie him, lead him home;
Tether him in the stable or lock him into the yard;
Where faces all day long
Gaze, gape, gasp at him and will not go away.

◇◇◇

Poem

W. Carlos Williams

AS the cat
climbed over
the top of

the jamcloset
first the right
forefoot

carefully
then the hind
stepped down

into tho pit of
the empty
flowerpot.

o o o o

Birches

Robert Frost

WIIEN I see birches bend to left and right
Across the lines of straighter darker trees,
I like to think some boy's been swinging them.
But swinging doesn't bend them down to stay
As ice-storms do. Often you must have seen them
Loaded with ice a sunny winter morning
After a rain. They click upon themselves
Ao the breeze rises, and turn many-coloured
As the stir cracks and crazes their enamel.
Soon the sun's warmth makes them shed crystal shells
Shattering and avalanching on the snow-crust—
Such heaps of broken glass to sweep away
You'd think the inner dome of heaven had fallen.
They are dragged to the withered bracken by the load,
And they seem not to break; though once they are
    bowed

So low for long, they never right themselves:
You may see their trunks arching in the woods
Years afterwards, trailing their leaves on the ground
Like girls on hands and knees that throw their hair
Before them over their heads to dry in the sun.
But I was going to say when Truth broke in
With all her matter-of-fact about the ice-storm
I should prefer to have some boy bend them
As he went out and in to fetch the cows—
Some boy too far from town to learn baseball,
Whose only play was what he found himself,
Summer or winter, and could play alone.
One by one he subdued his father's trees
By riding them down over and over again
Until he took the stiffness out of them,
And not one but hung limp, not one was left
For him to conquer. He learned all there was
To learn about not launching out too soon
And so not carrying the tree away
Clear to the ground. He always kept his poise
To the top branches, climbing carefully
With the same pains you use to fill a cup
Up to the brim, and even above the brim.
Then he flung outward, feet first, with a swish,
Kicking his way down through the air to the ground.
So was I once myself a swinger of birches.
And so I dream of going back to be.
It's when I'm weary of considerations,
And life is too much like a pathless wood
Where your face burns and tickles with the cobwebs
Broken across it, and one eye is weeping
From a twig's having lashed across it open.
I'd like to get away from earth awhile
And then come back to it and begin over.

May no fate wilfully misunderstand me
And half grant what I wish and snatch me away
Not to return. Earth's the right place for love:
I don't know where it's likely to go better.
I'd like to go by climbing a birch tree,
And climb black branches up a snow-white trunk
Toward heaven, till the tree could bear no more,
But dipped its top and set me down again.
That would be good both going and coming back.
One could do worse than be a swinger of birches.

◇◇◇◇

A Cat

Edward Thomas

SHE had a name among the children,
But no one loved though someone owned
Her, locked her out of doors at bedtime
And had her kittens duly drowned

In Spring, nevertheless, this cat
Ate blackbirds, thrushes, nightingales,
And birds of bright voice and plume and
    flight,
As well as scraps from neighbours' pails.

I loathed and hated her for this;
One speckle on a thrush's breast
Was worth a million such; and yet
She lived long, till God gave her rest.

◇◇◇◇

The Ballad of the Carpenters

L. A. G. Strong

AN ancient woman met with me,
Her voice was silver as her hair,
Her wild black eyes were certainly
The strangest I have seen.
She told a tale of carpenters
Who laboured for a queen.

'I had an island in a lake,
A wide lake, a quiet lake
Of sweet security.
I called them to me by the lake,
And they came gladly for my sake,—
My seven singing carpenters,
To build a house for me.

'They brought the hammer and the nails,
The pegs, the twine, the chisel blade,
The saw and whizzing plane.
They brought good share of timber wood,
Of resin wood, sweet smelling wood
Split kindly to the grain.
They brought them all for love of me;
They did not seek for gain.

'They built a house of singing wood,—
The white wood, the splendid wood,—
And made it snug around.
Their hammers on the ringing wood.
Made all the lake resound.

'The tench stirred dimly in his dream,
The glowing carp, the silly bream
Could hear the muffled sound.

'But someone grudged the fragrant wood
And sent a storm upon my house,
A black flood, a silver flood
Of wind and stinging rain.
The waters writhed in hissing rage,
The yelling wind, the rain-pocked waves
Rose in a hurricane.

'The slaty waves foamed hillock high,
The thunder pranced about the sky,
The lightning's bare and crooked fang
Gleamed where the cloud-lip curled.

'And when the calm came, and the peace
Of wind's cease and water's cease,
My house and seven carpenters
Had vanished from the world.'

<><><>

Can It Be ?

Stevie Smith

CAN it be, can it be
That beasts are of various bravery,
Some brave by nature, some not at all,
Some trying to be against a fall?

I saw a cat. Beside a lily tank,
Paved level with the grass, she stood, this cat,
Considering her leap.
Three times she backed for jumping, gathered tight
(So tight, thought landed her already over)
And did not jump. And then,

After a pause, as scolding humanly
'Not nervy, eh? We'll see'
She jumped. And what a jump that was!
Quite twice as long
And high
As it need be,
Now why
Did this cat jump at all, so force herself?
There was a path around the tank,
She could have walked.

Can it be, can it be
That beasts are of various bravery,
Some simply brave, some not, some taking thought
(Most curiously) to cast themselves aloft?

◇◇◇

The Man in the Moon stayed up Too Late

J. R. R. Tolkien

THERE is an inn, a merry old inn
     beneath an old grey hill,
And there they brew a beer so brown
That the Man in the Moon himself came down
     one night to drink his fill.

The ostler has a tipsy cat
     that plays a five-stringed fiddle;
And up and down he runs his bow,
Now squeaking high, now purring low,
     now sawing in the middle.

The landlord keeps a little dog
    that is mighty fond of jokes;
When there's good cheer among the guests,
He cocks an ear at all the jests
    and laughs until he chokes.

They also keep a horned cow
    as proud as any queen;
But music turns her head like ale,
And makes her wave her tufted tail
    and dance upon the green

And O! the row of silver dishes
    and the store of silver spoons!
For Sunday there's a special pair,
And these they polish up with care
    on Saturday afternoons.

The Man in the Moon was drinking deep,
    and the cat began to wail;
A dish and a spoon on the table danced,
The cow in the garden madly pranced,
    and the little dog chased his tail.

The Man in the Moon took another mug,
    and then rolled beneath his chair;
And there he dozed and dreamed of ale,
Till in the sky the stars were pale,
    and dawn was in the air.

The ostler said to his tipsy cat:
    'The white horses of the Moon,
They neigh and champ their silver bits;
But their master's been and drowned his wits,
    and the Sun'll be rising soon!'

So the cat on his fiddle played hey-diddle-diddle,
  a jig that would wake the dead:
He squeaked and sawed and quickened the tune,
While the landlord shook the Man in the Moon:
  'It's after three!' he said.

They rolled the Man slowly up the hill
  and bundled him into the Moon,
While his horses galloped up in rear,
And the cow came capering like a deer,
  and a dish ran up with a spoon.

Now quicker the fiddle went deedle-dum-diddle,
  the dog began to roar,
The cow and the horses stood on their heads;
The guests all bounded from their beds
  and danced upon the floor.

With a ping and a pong the fiddle-strings broke!
  the cow jumped over the Moon,
And the little dog laughed to see such fun,
And the Saturday dish went off at a run
  with the silver Sunday spoon.

The round Moon rolled behind the hill,
  as the Sun raised up her head.
She hardly believed her fiery eyes;
For though it was day, to her surprise
  they all went back to bed!

◇◇◇

India

W. J. Turner

THEY hunt, the velvet tigers in the jungle,
The spotted jungle full of shapeless patches—
Sometimes they're leaves, sometimes they're hanging
    flowers,
Sometimes they're hot gold patches of the sun:
They hunt, the velvet tigers in the jungle!

What do they hunt by glimmering pools of water,
By the round silver Moon, the Pool of Heaven—
In the striped grass, amid the barkless trees—
The stars scattered like eyes of beasts above them!

What do they hunt, their hot breath scorching insects,
Insects that blunder blindly in the way,
Vividly fluttering—they also are hunting,
Are glittering with a tiny ecstasy!

The grass is flaming and the trees are growing,
The very mud is gurgling in the pools,
Green toads are watching, crimson parrots flying,
Two pairs of eyes meet one another glowing—
They hunt, the velvet tigers in the jungle.

◇◇◇◇

Good Taste

Christopher Logue

TRAVELLING, a man met a tiger, so . . .
He ran. The tiger ran after him
Thinking: How fast I run . . . But

The road thought: How long I am . . . Then,
They came to a cliff, yes, the man
Grabbed at an ash root and swung down

Over its edge. Above his knuckles, the tiger.
At the foot of the cliff, its mate. Two mice,
One black, one white, began to gnaw the root.

And by the traveller's head grew one
Juicy strawberry, so . . . hugging the root
The man reached out and plucked the fruit.

How sweet it tasted!

◇—◇—◇

Hawthorn White

Charles Causley

HAWTHORN white, hawthorn red
Hanging in the garden at my head
Tell me simple, tell me true
When comes the winter what must I do?

I have a house with chimneys four
I have a silver bell on the door,
A single hearth and a single bed.
  Not enough, the hawthorn said.

I have a lute, I have a lyre
I have a yellow cat by my fire,
A nightingale to my tree is tied.
  That bird looks sick, the hawthorn sighed.

I write on paper pure as milk
I lie on sheets of Shantung silk,
On my green breast no sin has snowed.
   You'll catch your death, the hawthorn crowed.

My purse is packed with a five-pound note
The watchdogs in my garden gloat.
I blow the bagpipe down my side.
   Better blow your safe, the hawthorn cried.

My pulse is steady as my clock
My wits are wise as the weathercock.
Twice a year we are overhauled.
   It's Double Summer-Time! the hawthorn called.

I have a horse with wings for feet
I have chicken each day to eat.
When I was born the church-bells rang.
   Only one at a time, the hawthorn sang.

I have a cellar, I have a spread
The bronze blood runs round my bulkhead:
Why is my heart as light as lead?
   Love is not there, the hawthorn said.

◇◇◇◇

Cat

Eleanor Farjeon

   Cat!
   Scat!
Atter her, atter her,
Sleeky flatterer,
Spitfire chatterer,

Scatter her, scatter her
  Off her mat!
  Wuff!
  Wuff!
  Treat her rough!
Git her, git her,
Whiskery spitter!
Catch her, catch her,
Green-eyed scratcher!
  Slathery
  Slithery
  Hisser,
  Don't miss her!
Run till you're dithery,
  Hithery
  Thithery
  Pfitts! Pfitts!
  How she spits!
  Spitch! Spatch!
  Can't she scratch!
Scritching the bark
Of the sycamore-tree,
She's reached her ark
And's hissing at me
  Pfitts! Pfitts!
  Wuff! Wuff!
  Scat,
  Cat!
  That's
  That!

◇◇◇

in Just-

e. e. cummings

in Just-
spring when the world is mud-
luscious the little
lame balloonman

whistles far and wee

and eddieandbill come
running from marbles and
piracies and it's
spring

when the world is puddle-wonderful

the queer
old balloonman whistles
far and wee
and bettyandisbel come dancing

from hop scotch and jump-rope and

it's
spring
and
       the

          goat-footed

balloonMan whistles
far
and
wee

❖❖❖❖

The Runaway

Robert Frost

ONCE when the snow of the year was beginning to
    fall,
We stopped by a mountain pasture to say, 'Whose
    colt?'
A little Morgan had one forefoot on the wall,
The other curled at his breast. He dipped his head
And snorted at us. And then he had to bolt.
We heard the miniature thunder where he fled,
And we saw him, or thought we saw him, dim and
    grey,
Like a shadow against the curtain of falling flakes.
'I think the little fellow's afraid of the snow.
He isn't winter-broken. It isn't play
With the little fellow at all. He's running away.
I doubt if even his mother could tell him, "Sakes,
It's only weather." He'd think she didn't know!
Where is his mother? He can't be out alone.'
And now he comes again with clatter of stone,
And mounts the wall again with whited eyes
And all his tail that isn't hair up straight.
He shudders his coat as if to throw off flies.
'Whoever it is that leaves him out so late,
When other creatures have gone to stall and bin,
Ought to be told to come and take him in.'

◇◇◇

The Singing Cat

Stevie Smith

IT was a little captive cat
  Upon a crowded train
His mistress takes him from his box
  To ease his fretful pain.

Sho holds him tight upon her knee
  The graceful animal
And all the people look at him
  He is so beautiful.

But oh he pricks and oh he prods
  And turns upon her knee
Then lifteth up his innocent voice
  In plaintive melody.

He lifteth up his innocent voice
  He lifteth up, he singeth
And to each human countenance
  A smile of grace he bringeth.

He lifteth up his innocent paw
  Upon her breast he clingeth
And everybody cries, Behold
  The cat, the cat that singeth.

He lifteth up his innocent voice
  He lifteth up, he singeth
And all the people warm themselves
  In the love his beauty bringeth.

◇◇◇◇

School's Out

Hal Summers

FOUR o'clock strikes,
There's a rising hum,
Then the doors fly open,
The children come.

With a wild cat-call
And a hop-scotch hop
And a bouncing ball
And a whirling top,

Grazing of knees,
A hair-pull and a slap,
A hitched up satchel,
A pulled down cap,

Bully boys reeling off,
Hurt ones squealing off,
Aviators wheeling off,
Mousy ones stealing off,

Woollen gloves for chilblains,
Cotton rags for snufflers,
Pigtails, coat-tails,
Tails of mufflers,

Machine gun cries,
A kennelful of snarlings
A hurricane of leaves,
A treeful of starlings,

Thinning away now
By some and some,
Thinning away, away,
All gone home.

◇◇◇◇

The Child is Father to the Man,
but with More Authority

Ogden Nash

ONCE there were some children and they were un-
    interested in chores,
And they never picked anything up or put anything
    back or brought anything in from out of
    doors.
They didn't want to take care of anything, just to play
    with it,
And their parents let them get away with it.
Little did they know that Nemesis
Was on the premises.
Their regrets were at first scant
When they were left alone on their island summer
    home because their parents were called away by the
    convalescence of a wealthy aunt.
They prepared to take advantage of nobody being
    around,
And this is what they found,
This is how they were hoist with their own petards,
There wasn't a deck with more than fifty-one cards,
And when they tried to play the handsome phonograph
    with which they were equipped,

The records were either lost, warped, or chipped,
There were bows but no arrows, and bats and gloves
    but no ball,
And the untethered rowboat had drifted beyond
    recall,
And when they were wet the only towels were those
    strewn on the bathroom floor where moisture
    lingers,
And when they were cold they couldn't light a fire
    because all the matches had been used by people
    seeing how far down they would burn without
    burning their fingers.
Such experiences certainly taught them a lesson, and
    when their parents returned to their native heath,
Why, the first thing these children did was to leave the
    window open so it rained in on the piano, and
    go to bed without brushing their teeth.

◇◇◇◇

Lazy Man's Song

Arthur Waley

(FROM THE CHINESE)

I COULD have a job, but am too lazy to choose it;
I have got land, but am too lazy to farm it.
My house leaks; I am too lazy to mend it.
My clothes are torn; I am too lazy to darn them.
I have got wine, but I am too lazy to drink;
So it's just the same as if my cup were empty.
I have got a lute, but am too lazy to play;
So it's just the same as if it had no strings.

My family tells me there is no more steamed rice;
I want to cook, but am too lazy to grind.
My friends and relatives write me long letters;
I should like to read them, but they're such a bother
    to open.
I have always been told that Hsi Shu-ych
Passed his whole life in absolute idleness.
But he played his lute and sometimes worked at his
    forge;
So even *he* was not so lazy as I.

❖❖❖

The Sloth

Theodore Roethke

IN moving clow hc has no Pccr.
You ask him something in his ear,
He thinks about it for a Year;

And, then, before he says a Word
There, upside down (unlike a Bird),
He will assume that you have Heard—

A most Ex-as-per-at-ing Lug.
But should you call his manner Smug,
He'll sigh and give his Branch a Hug;

Then off again to Sleep he goes,
Still swaying gently by his Toes,
And you just *know* he knows he knows.

❖❖❖

The Jervis Bay

Michael Thwaites

THE *Jervis Bay* was a liner in the proper days of peace
When ocean roads were wide and free and needed no
  police.
Of good but modest station, she had pride but no false
  airs,
Not built to win Blue Ribands, or inveigle millionaires.
With passengers above decks and cargo down below
And fourteen thousand tons of her, and fourteen knots
  or so,
From Sydney home to Tilbury, by Suez or the Cape,
She plied her trade and did her bit and craved for no
  escape.
Many the dusty afternoon she cleared Port Melbourne
  pier
With streamers fluttering down the wind like the
  maypole of the year,
And friends on shore grew smaller as the gap began to
  grow
And shouted farewells were lost, and the tugs let go,
And the choicer spirits mused a space, and the thirsty
  went below.

And soon by Queenscliff and the Point her lifting bow
  was seen,
Her funnels buff, her cabins white, her hull a sober
  green,
And officers passed importantly, and flappers looked
  around them,
And troubled mothers sought their young and scolded
  when they found them.

Here slouched a careless student; here, discreetly
    prosperous, strolled
The established man of business, who'd found his land
    of gold,
And there the embittered immigrant, who sowed his
    oats too old.
Many the steely morning she nosed the Channel fog,
Three days without a sight of the sun, off Eddystone
    by the log,
And the siren moaned its dread despair, and the
    passengers joked and swore,
And thought of people in England, and strained for the
    fabulous shore,
And a hundred different hopes were kindled, and
    dreams thought dead awoke,
And the slowest pulse quickened a beat, and another
    morning broke.
But nothing of this for the *Jervis Bay*; she worked
    with an eye on the clock,
With a job to do and a tide to catch to make the
    Tilbury Dock,
Until at last the tugs were fast and laid her along the quay,
And that was the run, and her duty done to the public
    and the Company.
Such was the sober decent life of the S.S. *Jervis Bay*
To end at last in the breaker's yard. But War had
    another way.

In London in Whitehall sat the Lords of the Admiralty
Whose solemn office and trust is the dominion of the sea.
They measured the foe, and the ocean miles, and
    gaping wants of war,
They counted their ships, and knew they had need of
    thousands on thousands more.

The dockyards hummed with new construction; and
    straightway into the slip
After the launching, the keel went down of another
    fighting ship.
Week after week they took the water, grey and trim
    and tough,
Corvettes, destroyers, trawlers, sloops—and still it was
    not enough.
So many a ship of peaceful purpose was called to the
    tasks of war,
Was manned and armed and made anew for work
    unguessed before,
Came quietly into the dockyard and, converted,
    slipped away,
Yacht, trawler, ferry, liner, tramp. So came the
    Jervis Bay.

To Messrs Jones and Jubb she came, on the beating
    banks of Clyde,
And there in the dockyard's whelming din the civil
    liner died.
Down came the managers and draughtsmen, and the
    Admiralty Overseer,
With coats and plans and bowler hats and a brisk
    to-business air,
With 'Yes, quite so . . .' and 'What about . . .' and
    'Here's what I suggest,'
'The guns go here—the drawing's clear—we'll soon
    decide the rest.'
Down came the dockyard mateys like locusts on the
    land,
The welders, fitters, joiners, a shambling happy band,
The plumbers and the shipwrights, the electricians
    came,

The riveters, the painters, the host no man can name.
They came in caps and oily coats with bags of tools
and gear,
With drills and lamps and files and clamps and
newspapers and beer,
They shuffled up the gangplanks, they lolled along the
rails,
They stewed their tea on the galley stoves, they sat on
upturned pails,
They joked and ate and smoked and met, and jostled
each his neighbour,
Almost as though they did not know the dignity of
labour.
They diced and dozed and took their ease, and viewed
the job before them,
And found their way to nooks obscure before the
charge hand saw them.
And yet, by some organic change, she sprouted here a
gun
And there a bridge or rangefinder, till Presto! it was
done.
A dockyard matey working was a sight you rarely saw;
Yet when they left the *Jervis Bay* she was a ship of
war.

❖❖❖❖

The Garden Snail

Robert Wallace

THIS backyard
cousin
to the octopus

Sees
        through two filmy
            stems

On his head, at
    need
        can peer round

Corners, and
        so betrays his
            huge

Timidity. He
        moves on his
            single

Elastic foot
        seldom,
            preferring

Anonymity
        to danger,
            seems

Often to be
        meditating
            a very tough

Problem, likes
        green leaves
            and water.

Shyness
        is his prime
            virtue.

Though I have seen
    one,
        on a blue day

In summer,
    go climbing
        all afternoon

With his brown shell
    up the wobbly tall
        grass,

For a good
    look-round
        at the wide world.

❖❖❖

Lament, for Cocoa

John Updike

THE scum has come
    My cocoa's cold.
The cup is numb,
    And I grow old.

It seems an age
    Since from the pot
It bubbled, beige
    And burning hot—

Too hot to be
    Too quickly quaffed.
Accordingly,
    I found a draft

And in it placed
 The boiling brew
And took a taste
 Of toast or two.

Alas, time flies
 And minutes chill;
My cocoa lies
 Dull brown and still.

How wearisome!
 In likelihood,
The scum, once come,
 Is come for good.

◇◇◇◇

Song of the Bowmen of Shu

Ezra Pound

(FROM THE CHINESE)

HERE we are, picking the first fern-shoots
And saying: When shall we get back to our country?
Here we are because we have the Ken-nin for our
  foemen,
We have no comfort because of these Mongols.
We grub the soft fern-shoots,
When anyone says 'Return,' the others are full of
  sorrow.
Sorrowful minds, sorrow is strong, we are hungry and
  thirsty.
Our defence is not yet made sure, no one can let his
  friend return.

We grub the old fern-stalks.
We say: Will we be let to go back in October?
There is no ease in royal affairs, we have no comfort.
Our sorrow is bitter, but we would not return to our
   country.
What flower has come into blossom?
      Whose chariot? The General's.
Horses, his horses even, are tired. They were strong.
We have no rest, three battles a month
By heaven, his horses are tired.
The generals are on them, the soldiers are by them.
The horses are well trained, the generals have ivory
   arrows and quivers ornamented with fish-skin.
The enemy is swift, we must be careful.
When we set out, the willows were drooping with
   spring,
We come back in the snow,
We go slowly, we are hungry and thirsty,
Our mind is full of sorrow, who will know of our
   grief?

❖❖❖❖

The Old Pilot's Death

Donald Hall

HE discovers himself on an old airfield.
He thinks he was there before,
but rain has washed out the lettering of a sign.
A single biplane, all struts and wires,
stands in the long grass and wild flowers.
He pulls himself into the narrow cockpit
although his muscles are stiff
and sits like an egg in a nest of canvas.

He sees that the machine gun has rusted.
The glass over the instruments
has broken, and the red arrows are gone
from his gas gauge and his altimeter.
When he looks up, his propeller is turning,
although no one was there to snap it.
He lets out the throttle. The engine catches
and the propeller spins into the wind.
He bumps over holes in the grass,
and he remembers to pull back on the stick.
He rises from the land in a high bounce
which gets higher, and suddenly he is flying again.
He feels the old fear, and rising over the fields
the old gratitude. In the distance, circling
in a beam of late sun like birds migrating,
there are the wings of a thousand biplanes.
He banks and flies towards them.

◇◇◇◇

Jingle

Peter Champkin

I AM a poor man in a train,
I go to work and come again
And there is nothing in my brain
But go to work and come again.

I am a person in a crowd,
I cannot speak my thoughts aloud.
To the distinguished and the proud
I cannot speak my thoughts aloud.

I am a leader and my power
Can kill your leaders in an hour.
I am a poor man in a train,
I go to work and come again.

I am a person in a crowd,
I cannot speak my thoughts aloud.

⬦⬦⬦⬦

Blackbird

Christopher Leach

MY wife saw it first—
I was reading the evening paper.
Come and look, she said.

It was trying to drink
Where water had formed on a drain-cover.
It was shabby with dying
It did not move until I was very close—
Then hopped off, heavily,
Disturbing dead leaves.

We left water, crumbs.
It did not touch them
But waited among the leaves,
Silently.

This morning was beautiful:
Sunlight, other birds
Singing.

It was outside the door.
I picked it up
And it was like holding feathered air.
I wrapped what was left
Incongruously
In green sycamore leaves
And buried it near the tree,
Inches down.

This evening
I find it difficult to concentrate
On the paper, the news
Of another cosmonaut.

◇◇◇◇

Whale Hunt

Stanley Chapman

(TRANSLATED FROM THE FRENCH OF
JACQUES PRÉVERT)

OFF to catch a whale, we're off to catch a whale,
Said a wild man to his son
Ernest, dozing in the sun,
Off to catch a whale, we're off to catch a whale,
And you don't want to come.
Whatever can the trouble be?
Why should I go and catch a fish
That never troubles me?
Father, go and catch the whale
Yourself, you're sure to like the sail.

I'd rather stay at home with mum
And cousin Anthony.
So in his little whaleboat all alone the old man sailed
And the tide rolled out to sea. . . .

The old man's in the boat,
The young son's in the home,
The wild whale's in a temper,
And tiny cousin Tony's been upsetting all the cups,
All the careful cups of tea.

The storm was very bad,
The tea was very good,
And on his little stool little Ernest's feeling sad:
How I wish that I had sailed away with dad to catch a
     whale.
Whatever made me stay with mum and cousin
     Anthony?
We really might have caught a whale
And eaten it for tea.
But suddenly the handle turns.
Dripping like a fountain,
There's the old man out of breath
With the whale, big as a mountain.

He flings it on the table.
With its eyes like Betty Grable
It's the sort of whale that's rare these days.
Lifelessly the old man says:
Hurry up and carve it up,
I'm hungry, thirsty, need some grub.
But little Ernest stands up straight
And looks in the whites of his father's eyes,

In the whites of his father's bright blue eyes
As blue as the eyes of the blue-eyed whale:
Why should I carve a poor old fish
That never troubles me?
I don't want my share.

He throws the knife up in the air
But the whale has grabbed its handle
And attacked the wild old man
And stabbed him through his middle.
Oh, says tiny Tony, this reminds me of a riddle.

Ernest sits addressing many letters edged with black,
The mother wears a hat, a coat, a frock, all deadly
    black,
And the whale, with tear-stained eyes, looks around
    the shabby wreck
And sobs:
Whatever made me kill that wretched silly ass?
Now all the rest will chase me in their motor-boats
    and cars
And exterminate my race and my family tree.
Then, bursting into laughter in a strange and
    frightening way,
It swims to the door.
This is what it had to say
As it glided past the widow:
If anyone should ask,
For the whale, be polite,
Say it's just gone out to bask.
Tell them to be comfortable,
Tell them not to go,
Tell them I'll look in again in fifteen years or so. . . .

❖❖❖❖

The Nonny

James Reeves

THE Nonny-bird I love particularly;
    All day she chirps her joysome odes.
She rises perpendicularly,
    And if she goes too far, explodes.

❖❖❖❖

The Carpenter

Clifford Dyment

WITH a jack plane in his hands
My father the carpenter
Massaged the wafering wood,
Making it white and true.

He was skilful with his saws,
Handsaw, bowsaw, hacksaw,
And ripsaw with fishes' teeth
That chewed a plank in a second.

He was fond of silver bits,
The twist and countersink—
And the auger in its pit
Chucking shavings over its shoulder.

I remember my father's hands,
For they were supple and strong
With fingers that were lovers—
Sensuous strokers of wood:

He fondled the oak, the strong-man
Who holds above his head
A record-breaking lift
Of thick commingled boughs;

And he touched with his finger tips
Dark boards of elm and alder,
Spruce, and cherry for lathes
That turned all days to spring.

My father's hands were tender
Upon my tender head,
But they were massive on massive
Beam for building a house,

And delicate on the box wood
Leaning against the wall
As though placed there in a corner
For a moment and then forgotten,

And expert as they decoded
Archives unlocked by the axe—
The pretty medullary rays
Once jammed with a traffic of food

To a watched and desired tree
That he marked and felled in the winter,
The tracks of tractors smashing
The ground where violets grew,

Then bound in chains and dragged
To the slaughtering circular saw:
A railway dulcimer
Rang the passing bell

Of my father's loved ones,
Though there was no grief in him
Caressing the slim wood, hearing
A robin's piccolo song.

◇◇◇◇

The Song of the Dumb Waiter

James Reeves

WHO went to sleep in the flower-bed?
Who let the fire-dog out of the shed?

Who sailed the sauce-boat down the stream?
What did the railway-sleeper dream?

Who was it chopped the boot-tree down,
And rode the clothes-horse through the town?

ﺎﺎﺎﺎ

Idleness

Andrew Young

GOD, you've so much to do,
To think of, watch and listen to,
That I will let all else go by
And lending ear and eye
Help you to watch how in the combe
Winds sweep dead leaves without a broom;
And rooks in the spring-reddened trees

Restore their villages,
Nest by dark nest
Swaying at rest on the trees' frail unrest;
Or on this limestone wall,
Listening at ease, with you recall
How once these heavy stones
Swam in the sea as shells and bones;
And hear that owl snore in a tree
Till it grows dark enough for him to see;
In fact, will learn to shirk
No idleness that I may share your work.

◇◇◇◇

Fastitocalon

J. R. R. Tolkien

LOOK, there is Fastitocalon!
An island good to land upon,
    Although 'tis rather bare.
Come, leave the sea! And let us run,
Or dance, or lie down in the sun!
    See, gulls are sitting there!
                    Beware!
        Gulls do not sink.
There they may sit, or strut and prink:
Their part it is to tip the wink,
    If anyone should dare
    Upon that isle to settle,
Or only for a while to get
Relief from sickness or the wet,
    Or maybe boil a kettle.

Ah! foolish folk, who land on HIM,
And little fires proceed to trim
   And hope perhaps for tea!
It may be that His shell is thick,
He seems to sleep; but He is quick,
   And floats now in the sea
         With guile;
And when He hears their tapping feet,
Or faintly feels the sudden heat,
      With smile
      HE dives,
And promptly turning upside-down
He tips them off, and deep they drown,
   And lose their silly lives
     To their surprise.

     Be wise!
There are many monsters in the Sea,
But none so perilous as HE,
Old horny Fastitocalon,
Whose mighty kindred all have gone,
The last of the old Turtle-fish.
So if to save your life you wish
    Then I advise:
Pay heed to sailors' ancient lore,
Set foot on no uncharted shore!
    Or better still,
Your days at peace on Middle-earth
        In mirth
        Fulfil!

◇◇◇◇

With Half an Eye

Philip Hobsbaum

AT seven the sun that lit my world blew out
Leaving me only mist. Through which I probed
My way to school, guessed wildly at the sums
Whose marks on the board I couldn't even see.

They wanted to send me away to a special school.
I refused, and coped as best I could with half
The light lost in the mist, screwing my tears
Into my work, my gritted teeth, my writing—

Which crawled along and writhed. Think thoughts at
    will,
None of it comes across. Even now friends ask
'How do you read your writing?' The fact is, I don't;
Nobody could. I guess. But how would you

Like my world where parallels actually join,
Dimensions vary at sight? Once in a pub
I walked towards a sign marked gents over
A grating and crashed through the floor—

Well, it looked all right to me. Those steep stairs
People told me of later flattened to lines
In my half-world. The rest imagination
Supplied: when you've half a line you extend it.

The lenses drag their framework down my nose.
I still can't look strangers in the face,
Wilting behind a wall of glass at them.
It makes me look shifty at interviews.

I wake up with a headache, chew all day
Aspirins, go to bed dispirited,
Still with a dull pain somewhere in my skull,
And sleep. Then, in my dreams, the sun comes out.

⋄⋄⋄⋄

Lone Dog

Irene McLeod

I'M a loan dog, a keen dog, a wild dog and lone,
I'm a rough dog, a tough dog, hunting on my own!
I'm a bad dog, a mad dog, teasing silly sheep;
I love to sit and bay the moon and keep fat souls from
   sleep.

I'll never be a lap dog, licking dirty feet,
A sleek dog, a meek dog, cringing for my meat.
Not for me the fireside, the well-filled plate,
But shut door and sharp stone and cuff and kick and
   hate.

Not for me the other dogs, running by my side,
Some have run a short while, but none of them would
   bide.
O mine is still the lone trail, the hard trail, the best,
Wide wind and wild stars and the hunger of the quest.

INDEX TO FIRST LINES